A STEPPING-STONE BOOK

Sense of Direction

Up and Down and All Around

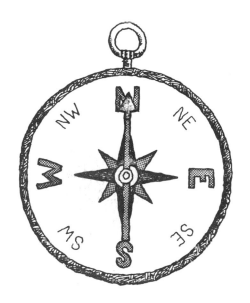

by VICKI COBB

pictures by CAROL NICKLAUS

Parents' Magazine Press · *New York*

CONTENTS

Chapter One
WHERE ARE YOU?

At this very moment, you know exactly where you are. There are several reasons why. You have been here before, so everything is familiar to you. You know how to get here. You know how to get from here to other places you may want to go.

Being lost is just the opposite from knowing where you are. Everything is strange. You don't remember how you got there and you can't find your way to places you do know. Being lost can be very frightening.

It's a good thing for us that there were a few people who were not afraid to go places no one had ever been before. If Christopher Columbus and others like him had stayed home, America might never have been discovered.

But explorers did not set out on journeys without knowing something about finding their way. They knew how to do a few things to keep track of where they were and where they had been. They knew how to make sure they kept going in the same direction and not in circles. They knew how to find their way home. Best of all, they knew how to tell other people how to get where they had been.

Some of the methods explorers used in discovering new lands can help you find your way in case you are ever lost. You can learn how to follow directions to get to places you have never been. You don't have to know how to drive a car, or pilot a ship or airplane to be an explorer. There may be woods, fields, caves, and ponds not far from where you live to be discovered by you. Maybe you can be the navigator on the next trip your family takes. You can find new places to go on the buses and subways of your town or city. All you need is a

compass, a map when one exists, and some
information about using them that you can get from
this book.

Chapter Two
YOUR BODY POINTS THE WAY

You may make journeys in your lifetime to many different places. You may go to the park down the street, or to the open seas, and some day you may even go to the moon. But no matter where you go, you have something with you that can help you find your way. It's your own body.

Your body can show you all the most important directions you need to know. It has a top and bottom to show you *up* and *down.* It has a front and back to show you *forward* and *backward.* It has

two sides that show you *right* and *left*. You can use your body to know where you are at this moment and to tell you which way to go.

The easiest directions to find on earth are up and down. The earth has a force called *gravity* that keeps you on the earth's surface. "Up" means away from the earth and "down" means toward the center of the earth.

Did you have to go up or down to get where you are right now? Some objects are higher than others. Can you name some things that are high—up—and some that are low—down? What part of a tree is up and what part is down?

In space, there is no gravity. Spacemen use their bodies to tell them up and down. In space, "up" means toward the head and "down" means toward the feet.

The direction "in front of you" means the way

you are facing. "Behind you" is the opposite direction. Unless you walk sideways like a crab, you usually face in the direction you are going. The direction behind you is usually where you have been. Of course, if you wanted to travel in the direction behind you, you could turn around and it would then be the direction in front of you. What is important is that your front and back give you *two* directions.

The two directions that seem hardest to learn are right and left. Perhaps this is because the right side of your body looks exactly like the left side, except that it is reversed.

It takes practice to learn right and left. You know if you are right-handed or left-handed, because you know which hand you use for writing and eating. Everything that is on the side of your left hand is in the direction "left" and everything on the side of your right hand is in the direction "right." When you are facing someone, that person's right hand is on the same side as your left hand.

Chapter Three
HOW TO MARK YOUR PLACE

When you know all the directions your body shows
you, you are ready to mark your place. Marking
your place means that you find a way of always
knowing where you are by the objects you see
around you. These objects are called *landmarks.*

A good landmark is something different enough to
stay in your mind. It can be a tree with a crooked
trunk, a river running through a valley, an arrow

13

painted on a rock, or a special kind of store on a corner. The position of a landmark is also important. Sometimes it may be in front of you, sometimes to your right or left.

Sometimes you can use more than one landmark to mark your place. You can say "My house is on the left of a red brick house and on the right of a grocery store and behind a large oak tree." What are the landmarks around your school and house? Can you name three landmarks for each place? What is the position of your school or house compared to these landmarks? Are they in front or in back, to the right or the left? They might even be above or below—up or down.

Landmarks can be used for telling how to get from one place to another. Suppose you wanted to tell someone how to get from your house to your school. You can use blocks or streets as landmarks to tell him how far to go. You might say, "Turn left when you leave the house, go three blocks and cross two streets." You can use buildings like fire houses or churches to tell your friend where to turn. You might say, "Turn left at the fire house" or "Turn right two blocks past the church." What directions would *you* give so anyone could find the way from your house to your school?

Chapter Four
LANDMARKS FOR EVERYONE

It is easy to find landmarks in cities or on well-marked trails through the woods. When people know the landmarks in a place, they can tell newcomers how to get around. But there are places on earth, like the middle of the ocean, where there are no landmarks. Everything looks the same in all directions.

Explorers and sailors needed a way to mark their places with something they could see, no matter where they were. They had to have a way of telling how far they had gone and which way to go. Fortunately, nature has given us what we need to find out where we are anywhere on earth. Nature's landmarks, however, are not on the ground. They are in the sky. People had the courage to wander far from home because they could always see the sun and the stars.

No one knows when people first started keeping track of the sun's path as it moved across the sky. It must have been about the same time people named the groups of stars that make patterns of tiny lights in the night sky. You can imagine how much comfort the sun and stars gave a traveler far from home. Even in strange and distant lands, at night he could see stars he knew, and during the day, the familiar sun.

For this reason, the sun and stars are good landmarks. There is only one problem. The sun and stars seem to be *moving*. How can you use the positions of the sun or stars to mark your place if their positions are always changing? How can you use the sun or stars to point a direction when the direction they point to is different from one moment to the next? The sun and stars could only be useful as landmarks for people moving on the earth's surface, when people finally understood just how they moved.

It took a long time for people to discover that the sun and stars are *not* really moving. It is the earth that moves. The earth is always spinning like a top and people on earth move with it as it spins. Since we cannot feel the earth moving, it *seems* as if the sun travels across the sky and the stars turn around a central point in the sky like a giant record on a turntable.

The movement of the earth is very regular. The sun and stars make their paths in the sky every twenty-four hours—once a day. The time of day is important when you use the sun or stars as landmarks.

Every day at noon, the sun is as high in the sky as it will get. If you stand outdoors on a sunny day at noon, your shadow points in a direction called *north.* You can remember which way is north at other times by finding a landmark your shadow points to.

19

When you are certain about which way is north, you also know three other directions. If north is directly in front of you, then *south* is behind you. *East* is to your right and *west* is to your left.

Next time you have a chance, look at the sun at noon and see if you can find north, south, east, and west. Then look for landmarks, so you can find these directions from the same spot any time you want to. What landmark can you find that is directly south of your house? Which direction do you see from your classroom window? In which direction do you travel when you go to school?

You can also use the stars to find north. All the stars in the sky seem to move very slowly during the night except for one that is in the center of all the others. This star is called the North Star. It isn't very bright, but you can find it by looking for a group of seven stars shaped like a spoon. These stars are called the "Big Dipper." The two stars that form the bowl of the dipper are called the "pointers"

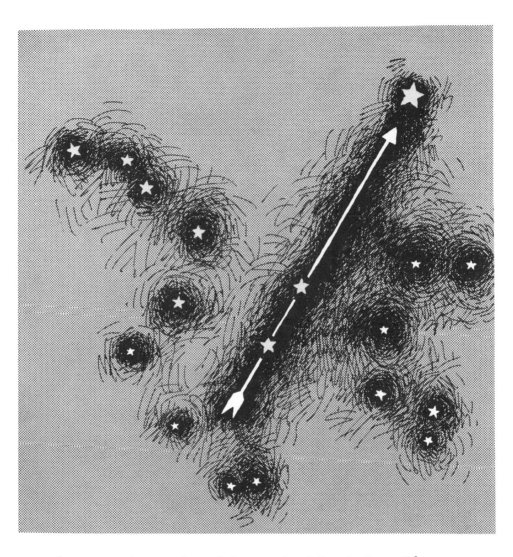

because they point right to the North Star. If you
draw an imaginary line along these pointers, the
next star in line is the North Star.

North, south, east, and west are important
directions when you travel along the surface of the
earth. Up and down are important directions for
submarine captains and airplane pilots. Pilots must
know how high they are so that they don't crash
into mountains and tall buildings. Submarine
captains must keep from crashing into the ocean
floor and into mountains under the sea.

People had to decide where up and down began
on earth so that they had a way of comparing

mountains and valleys on the uneven surface of the earth. They decided that up and down should be measured in feet above or below the surface of the ocean, which is called sea level.

The tallest point on earth is the top of Mount Everest, which is 29,028 feet, or almost six miles, above sea level. The lowest point is just over six miles beneath the surface of the ocean.

Submarines and airplanes have instruments that can tell them how far up or down they are.

Chapter Five
THE ROSE AND THE MAGIC NEEDLE

The only things a sailor sees in the middle of the ocean are the sea, the sky, and the line where they meet. This line is called the *horizon*. The horizon makes a giant circle around the ship which is at its center. Long ago, sailors depended on winds to move their ships. The winds that moved a ship came from many different directions on the horizon.

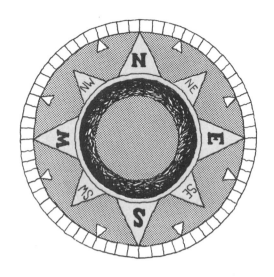

Navigators had to know more directions than north, south, east, and west. They found the directions in between by dividing the horizon like a pie into equal sections.

Sailors used a picture called a *wind rose* to divide the horizon. North and south are opposite points on the rose, as are east and west. The points between these four directions show the directions of many winds. What are the names of some of the directions between east and south in this picture of a wind rose? What are some between west and north?

If all the days were sunny and if all the nights were clear, sailors and explorers would never have to worry about finding the right directions. They would always have the sun and the stars and a wind rose to help them. But often the sky is cloudy and sometimes a ship might be tossed about in a storm for several days. By the time the sky has cleared, the captain might be lost. Unless, of course, there was another way of telling the direction in which they were going. The key to finding directions when the sky can not be seen is an ordinary looking brown stone called *magnetite.*

When an iron or steel needle is rubbed with magnetite, it acts in a strange way. If a string is tied around the middle and the needle is allowed to swing freely, when it stops swinging, it points in a north-south direction. You can see for yourself how this works. Rub one end of a magnet (which was made from magnetite) along a sewing needle. Don't rub back and forth, but keep stroking the needle in the same direction about twenty or thirty times. Tie some thread around the middle of the needle and hang it in a milk bottle or place the needle on a small cork floating in a bowl of water. (Don't use a metal bowl, and make sure there is no metal, except the needle, close by when you do this. Other metal will change the direction of the needle.) Take your magic needle to the place where you found north by the sun. Does the needle point north?

The modern compass is simply a magnetized needle that is free to turn above a wind rose. The

end of the needle that points north is usually colored, while the south-pointing end is unpainted metal.

A compass is easy to use. All you have to do to find north is to turn the compass so that the direction marked "N" on the rose is directly under the north-pointing end of the needle. Then all the other points on the rose will be pointing in the right directions.

It is fun to have a compass. You can carry one around with you and check your direction every once in a while.

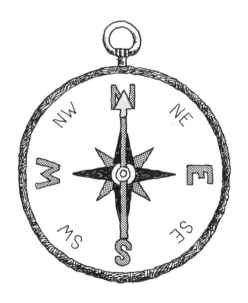

Chapter Six
HOW FAR BETWEEN LANDMARKS?

Finding your way depends on more than knowing which direction to go and which landmarks to look for. You also have to know how far you have gone.

Short distances, like the length of a room, are easy to measure with a ruler. But this kind of measuring tool is not useful for finding longer distances between towns and cities.

When people first started measuring longer distances, they may have counted the steps they took going from one place to another. They may have used traveling time by horseback or oxcart to measure distances. One city could be three hours away by oxcart or one hour away by horseback. But

these ways of measuring distances had some
problems. Many things could happen on a journey,
which could make traveling time faster or slower,
and counting steps certainly didn't make a trip
very interesting. Besides, some people take longer
steps than others.

Then someone invented a way of measuring distances with a counter attached to a wheel of a wagon. The counter kept track of the number of times the wheel of the wagon went around. If you knew how many times a wheel went around and you also knew the distance around the rim of the wheel, you could figure out how far you had gone.

The *odometer* on the dashboard of a car is a modern invention something like the early counters attached to wagon wheels. An odometer measures the miles you travel by keeping track of the number of times the wheels go around.

Measuring distances at sea was a more difficult problem than measuring distances on land. Ships do not have wheels that roll along a surface. Sailors had to figure out how far they had traveled by knowing *how fast* they were going.

Long ago, sailors found the speed of a ship with a long rope, a log, and a sand glass that measured half a minute. They tied knots in the rope equal distances apart. They wound the knotted rope on a large spool and put it near the side of the ship. They tied a log with a heavy weight on one side to the end of the rope. When they wanted to know how fast they were going, they threw the log into

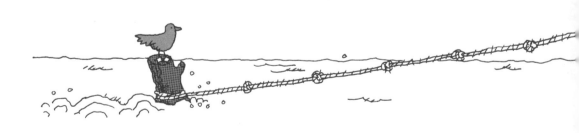

the water. The weight made the log stay in one place.

As the ship moved away from the log, the rope on the spool unwound. A sailor would turn over the sand glass and, as the sand ran out, count the knots as they passed over the side of the ship. By knowing the number of knots and the distance between each knot, he could figure out how far the ship had gone

in half a minute. Then it was easy to figure out how far the ship had gone in an hour.

The speed of a ship was measured in *knots* and written down in a book called the *log record*. Usually, sailors measured the ship's speed every two hours. A modern ship's speed is measured with a more complicated kind of knotted rope and log, but the terms "log record" and "knots," which now means "miles per hour," are still used today.

Hour	Course	Speed	Wind	Comments
0800	90°	6 K	NNE	
0830	90°	6½K	NNE	Saw a school of porpoises.
0900	95°	6½K	NE	Getting cloudy.
0930	95°	5 K	NE	Rain !

Ship's Log

Chapter Seven
TELLING OTHERS THE WAY

It is one thing for explorers and navigators to be able to travel to unknown places and find their way home again. It is another thing to be able to tell others how to get there, too. The invention that helps tell others the way is a map.

A map is a picture that shows the positions of landmarks. Maps can show many different things. Maps can show where to find parks and beaches and the roads to take to get you there. Some maps show where one nation ends and another begins. Maps can show the shape of a coastline and where you can find different cities and towns and rivers and lakes. These cities and towns, rivers and lakes are in the same direction from each other on the map as they really are on earth.

Most maps use symbols that stand for different landmarks. Symbols save space so that maps can give more information. The picture shows some symbols you might see on a road map.

One of the best ways to learn about maps is to draw one yourself. You can make a map of your own neighborhood. In cities and towns, streets have names or numbers, or both. Buildings on a street are also numbered. The name of a street and the number of a building is called an address. When you make a map of your neighborhood, be sure to

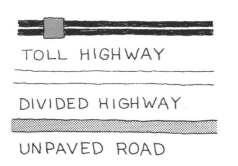
TOLL HIGHWAY

 INTERSTATE HIGHWAY

DIVIDED HIGHWAY

 U.S. HIGHWAY

UNPAVED ROAD

 STATE HIGHWAY

 STATE CAPITAL

 COVERED BRIDGE

 PRIVATE AIRPORT

 STATE FOREST

 LARGE AIRPORT

 CAMPGROUND

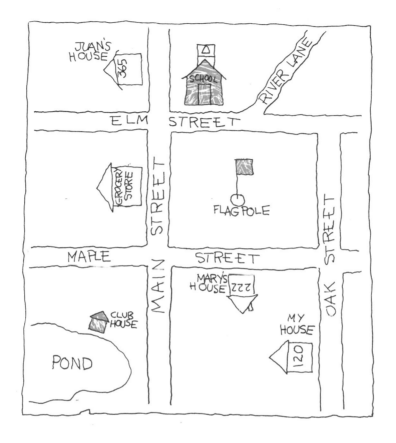

give the names of all the streets and show the
numbers of some of the buildings.

Your map might look something like the one on
this page.

The most important information you can get from
maps is the direction and distance you must go to
get from one landmark to another. Some maps show

directions with a small wind rose in a corner. Usually, north is at the top of a map, south is at the bottom, east is on the right, and west is on the left.

Here is a map of Illinois and part of the states around it. What is the name of the state east of Illinois? What state is to its south? What state is to its west? What lake is in the northwest corner of Illinois? What river forms the western edge of the state?

Maps are drawn so that one inch on the map stands for a certain number of miles on the ground. The number of miles an inch stands for is called the "scale of miles" and it is usually printed on the map. In the map of Illinois one inch equals 50 miles. That is the scale of miles. Landmarks that are two inches from each other on the map are 100 miles apart on earth. Use a ruler to find out how far Chicago is from St. Louis. How far is Peoria from Springfield?

Chapter Eight
READING A MAP

A good time to read a map is when you are planning a trip. Then you can be sure of the way before you start to travel. You will know ahead of time which landmarks to look for and where to turn.

The first thing to find on a map is your starting point. Look for large landmarks that you know are near your city or town. A body of water is easy to see on a map and is a good landmark to look for. On the map of Illinois, what landmark marks the place of Chicago? What landmark would you look for on a map that shows your city or town?

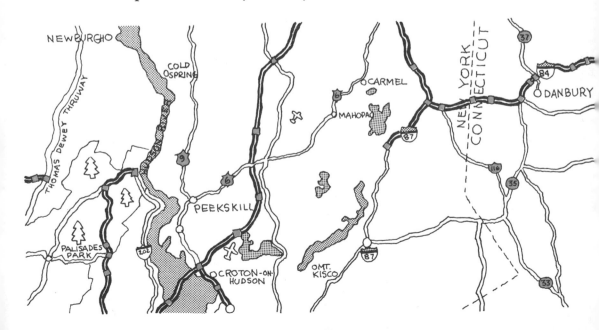

The next thing to find on a map is the place you
are going to. You can do this the same way you
found your starting point, by looking for landmarks.
Or you can look in the direction you must travel to
get there. Suppose you wanted to go from St. Louis
to Charleston, Illinois. You have to travel in a
northeasterly direction to get there. Move your
finger on the map on page 41 in a northeasterly
direction from St. Louis. Can you find Charleston on
the way?

The last thing to look for is the road to travel.
Road maps show the differences between major
highways and smaller roads.

Bus maps show the routes of all the buses in a
city or town.

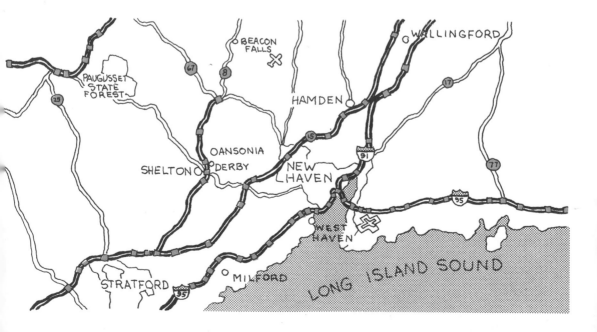

Look for routes on a map that connect your starting point with the place you want to go. There may be several ways of getting there. Then choose the way you want to go, depending on the kind of trip you want to take. You might choose one route because it is faster, or prettier, or more direct than another.

While you are traveling, a map can tell you where to change directions and which way to turn. Suppose you are traveling north. Which direction do you go when you make a left turn? Take a look at the map on pages 42 and 43. Move your finger over the map in a northerly direction. Then make a left turn with your finger. Are you going west?

Now suppose you are traveling south. In which direction are you going if you make a left turn? How would you hold a map so that a left turn goes east when you are traveling south? A good rule to follow when you are traveling is to hold a map so that the direction you are going in is on top. That way, a right turn on the map will show you where to make a right turn on the road.

Chapter Nine
WHERE ON EARTH . . .?

Long ago, people wondered about the size and shape
of the earth. They knew the earth was large because
travelers could go in the same direction for many
days and, when they looked out to sea, it seemed
endless.

Some people thought the earth was flat because
the sea looked flat. It was finally proved that the
earth is really shaped like a ball. It seems flat
because it is so large. A line dividing the earth in
half is 25,000 miles long. People are so small,
compared to the size of the earth, that they cannot
see its curved surface unless they go far out into
space.

Explorers and navigators found that the earth's
surface is covered with water and land masses. In

order to show where land and water are on earth, mapmakers drew a map on a ball that has the same shape as the earth. This kind of map of the world is called a *globe.*

Like other maps, a globe shows directions. A point near the center of the top is the North Pole. The North Pole points directly toward the North Star. The direction "north" on a globe means "toward the North Pole."

On the opposite side of the globe, near the center of the bottom, is the South Pole. As you might expect, the direction "south" means "toward the South Pole."

NORTH POLE

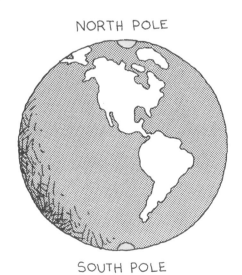

SOUTH POLE

CLOCKWISE   COUNTERCLOCKWISE

When you travel north or south on earth you can go only as far as the Poles. When you are at the North Pole, the only direction you can go is south.

The directions east and west have a different meaning on a globe than on a flat map. On a globe, one point on earth may be east or west of another point, depending on which way you go there. Japan, for example, is west of the United States if you go there from California. But it is east of the United States if you go there through Europe. West means moving around the earth in a *clockwise* direction and east means moving in a *counterclockwise* direction.

In order to find any landmark on earth, mapmakers have divided the earth with two sets of

imaginary lines. They draw these lines on a globe so
you can see where they are. One set of lines tells
you how far east or west you are. These lines, called
meridians of longitude, are like the lines you see
between the pieces of a peeled orange. Meridians go
from top to bottom around the globe.

Looking down from the top of a globe, you see
that all the meridians meet at the North Pole and

divide the earth into wedges that are all the same
size. Mapmakers have chosen one meridian as the
point where east and west begin. This line, called
the *prime meridian,* passes through Greenwich,
England. The half of the earth that is left of the
prime meridian is west longitude and the right half
is east longitude.

Look at the globe in the picture. Can you find
the prime meridian? Is the United States west or
east longitude?

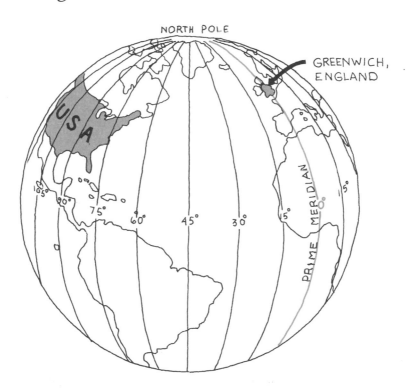

The other set of imaginary lines dividing the
earth crosses the meridians to form a network. These
lines, called *parallels of latitude,* tell you how far
north or south you are. Parallels go from left to
right, or right to left, around the globe.

The *equator* is the line that divides the north half
of the earth or *northern hemisphere* from the *southern
hemisphere.* The United States is in the northern
hemisphere and Brazil is in the southern
hemisphere.

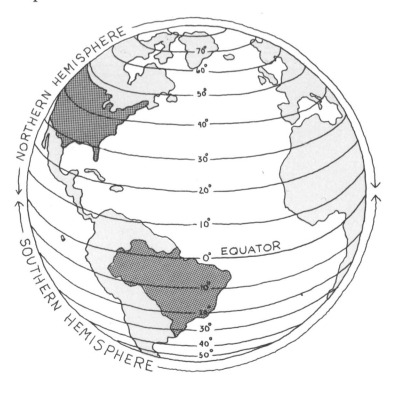

The parallels of latitude north and south of the equator are always the same distance apart. If you looked down on these parallels from the North Pole, they would look like the lines made by onion rings. The parallels in the northern hemisphere are called north latitude and those in the southern hemisphere are called south latitude.

Look at the globe on page 54 and see if you can name some countries that have north latitude and some that have south latitude.

The network formed by meridians and parallels covers the earth. Each meridian and parallel has a number. When you know the number of the meridian and parallel you know exactly where you are on earth. Washington, D.C., for example is located at the point where the 39th parallel north latitude crosses the 77th meridian west longitude. No other place on earth has the same latitude and longitude.

As you might expect, it is very important for ship captains and airplane pilots to know exactly where they are at all times. Navigators have the job of finding the latitude and longitude of their ship or plane whenever they are on a journey. They are specially trained to be able to find their position by using delicate instruments.

Chapter Ten
SENSING DIRECTIONS

Navigators use stars and maps and compasses to help find their way on earth. But their usefulness depends on certain senses all people have in their bodies. Stars and maps and compasses cannot help you find your way unless you can see them. The sense of sight is very important in finding directions.

There is another sense in your body that is even more important than sight for finding your way. It is the sense of balance that is in the part of your ears deep inside your head. You can find out how important this sense is with a simple experiment. Stand on one side of a large room and decide on a spot you will walk to on the other side. Have a friend blindfold you. Can you walk directly to that spot even if you can't see? Can you walk in a straight line?

Repeat the experiment this way. Keep the blindfold on, but have your friend spin you around

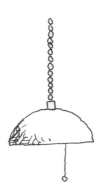

a few times before you try to walk across the room.
Now can you walk directly to the place where you
want to go? Do you walk in a straight line? A dizzy
person loses the sense of balance and the sense of
direction.

Hearing can also be important for finding directions. You can use sound to tell you where to go. Here is a good experiment you can do outdoors. Have a friend blindfold you. Then tell the friend to

go some place not too far away and blow a whistle in short blasts. See if you can walk directly to your friend as you listen to the sound.

Sometimes, if you are lost, a sound can be more

important than knowing direction. Many people
have found their way out of the woods by listening
for a highway or a stream and walking toward the
sound.

You use your senses of sight and balance and hearing to find your way from one landmark to another. You use them to find north, south, east, and west. You need your senses to travel a straight line and to turn. If you walk around with a compass, you can learn how to use your senses better to find directions. Every once in a while, make a guess about the direction in which you are facing. Check your direction with a compass. Soon you will have a pretty good idea which way is north.

A good sense of direction can keep you from getting lost. It will also help you to find new places to go in your neighborhood, town, or city, in the United States, and some day, in other parts of the world.

INDEX